FEAR IN THE FOREST

VOLUME 2

ETHAN HAYES

CONTENTS

CHAPTER 1
TERRIFYING GRAY THING

When I was sixteen I was camping in the woods with some friends for the weekend. We were all having a really good time as camping was one of our most favorite things to do and something we did all the time. Where we grew up there really wasn't much else for young kids or teenagers to do in the town and life got pretty boring. So, more often than not, especially in the summertime, we would all get together and drive out to a local spot that used to be a summer camp way back in the nineteen fifties. This all happened in the eighties so that seemed like a lifetime ago, even then. It was private property and illegal to be there without permission but we weren't loud or rowdy and didn't cause any trouble.

We didn't drink or do drugs and so even on the few and very rare occasions that we would get caught out there, normally a security person would come and tell us we shouldn't be there and needed to be gone by morning. Our parents didn't know that that's where we were and because we were all females and all best friends, we would just tell our parents that we were at one of the other one's houses and that was that. It always worked and we hadn't ever been caught by our parents being out there. We had been going to that old, abandoned camp for a little over a year at that point and we were just starting to become familiar with everything there and all of the land and stuff. It was a place to be alone and to feel like we were grown up. We always camped outside and didn't really go in the cabins. There was no electricity and the plumbing didn't work inside of the ten or twelve cabins but they were in almost pristine condition, despite having been completely abandoned for about thirty years. There was wildlife in most of them though and we didn't even want to think about what else. We got our kicks off of horror movies too and it would sometimes get really scary at night.

Not only was the old camp located in the middle of some really dense and desolate woods but it was also way out in the middle of nowhere. Our friend Ronnie's sister would drive us out there sometimes, when we had enough money between the four of us to chip in for either her booze or her cigarettes and then we would just hitch a ride home. So, it was just another summer night and we were laying in the middle of the lake on one of the docks and looking at the stars. There weren't as many out that night as there usually were at that time of year and the moon was barely a sliver in the sky. There was enough light though, somehow, and we were having a good time when all of a sudden we started hearing really loud clicking noises, sort of like someone incessantly clucking their tongue at us, but it sounded like it was coming from all over the place. We all immediately stopped laughing and giggling and got quiet. We had no idea what it could have been but we were immediately scared. The symphony of clicks and clucks lasted for about fifteen minutes but while it was happening we were all too afraid to move let alone get back in the water and swim back to shore to investigate. Eventually though it died down and then there was nothing but silence. Looking back on it now it was as if everything was way too silent and quiet but back then we just laughed at how scary the noises had left us and went right back to looking at the stars and gossiping like the normal teenage girls that we were.

Suddenly something red that looked like it was on fire blazed across the sky, and then one right behind that. It was in no way, shape or form a shooting star and I say that because I remember seeing shooting stars all the time back then because the sky was always so clear around those parts and these things looked nothing like them. My friends and I jumped up again as we watched the blazing balls of fire shoot through the sky and disappear. They looked like they were falling fast from the sky and as we turned around to see which direction they were going in, it seemed to us like they were falling into the woods. One right after the other they fell and we counted eight altogether. Our suspicion that they were landing in the woods was confirmed when we saw over our shoulders that they seemed to be falling through the trees about a hundred feet from where we were on the docks. We were all really scared but knew that we had to get out of the water and back on to the relative safety of dry land again. We all jumped in and made our way back to shore and back to our little camp as fast as we possibly could.

We didn't dare start a fire lest we risk someone telling us we had to leave and we used flashlights for most of our illumination along the trails and also as we sat there around our tents talking some more. We hadn't seen or heard anything strange the whole time we were making our way, cautiously, back to our tents but we were all terrified and wondering what in the hell had been falling from the sky. We thought that whatever the objects were that they were on fire but once they seemed to drop into the woods there weren't any actual fires that had sprung up anywhere though. We finally called it a night at around one in the morning. We had discussed going to investigate but decided to wait until the morning before we did so. It was around two thirty when I woke up to go pee and walked to the edge of the woods that were surrounding our little makeshift campsite and I was startled by the sight of my one friend, Josie, already awake and standing there, facing the woods. She didn't seem to be doing anything like going to the bathroom or anything so I went up to her and asked her if she was okay and what she was doing. She didn't respond and was staring straight ahead into the woods, her mouth was moving but she wasn't actually saying anything. She didn't turn to look at me and she wasn't blinking either. It was the creepiest thing I had ever seen, up to that point in my life anyway. I shook her and when she still didn't respond I slapped her, hard, across her face. That did the trick and she immediately put her hand up to her cheek, turned and looked at me wide eyed and asked me what I had done that for. I told her she was being weird and not answering me and she swore she had only been out there going pee. She was angry and stormed off, going back into her tent. I didn't know what was going on but I was exhausted so I went and did my business and turned to go back to my own tent to go back to sleep. I heard rustling in the bushes.

I turned back towards the woods and saw something standing there, between two trees and when I shined my flashlight on it I almost screamed. It was hideous and terrifying and I didn't know what in the world it was. It was at least ten feet tall, had a gigantic and bulbous head that was sort of in the shape of a light bulb, and the biggest, darkest black eyes I had ever seen. I stood there and my mouth was still open because of sheer terror and the inability for my mind to grasp what it was I had come face to face with. Its arms were extremely long and thin as were its legs. It just stood there, staring at me. Its skin was a bluish gray color and it didn't even flinch at the light I was shining into its face. cIt lifted one long and gnarled looking finger and pointed at me. I immediately lowered my light without even thinking about it. It had forced me to do that, of that I was sure and that scared me too. Suddenly there were others, all stepping out of random places behind trees and bushes, all walking up to stand with the one I had initially seen. They were all different shapes and sizes but they all had the same giant, bulbous head and humongous black eyes. They all had the same color skin too. They started walking towards me. For at least a minute I was too scared to move but eventually my adrenaline kicked in and I turned to run. The clicking and clucking noises my friends and I had heard earlier while we were lying on the dock started again and once again it was like it was coming from everywhere all at once. I was crying by the time I got back to my tent. I got fully back into my tent before I realized I should have woken up my friends and none of them seemed to be awake because none of them were making any noise at all. I looked out of my tent to see where the creatures were but didn't see anything. I got under my blanket, closed my eyes really tight and started to pray.

It seemed like as soon as I did that the noise stopped all at once and just as suddenly as it had started. I slowly opened my eyes and peered out from under my blanket and once I didn't see or hear anything after a minute or two, I decided to look out of my tent again and see if the creatures were there or if my friends were awake. I slowly crawled to the front of my tent and looked out. There, surrounding my friend Josie's tent, were five creatures. It didn't seem like she was awake because she wasn't moving around inside or screaming. I was sure if she had seen what I was seeing she would be screaming non stop and waking up the whole town. Not that I would blame her. They were at least ten feet away from me or more and I was about to lose my mind and just start bellowing out for help. The creatures had no mouths, I forgot to mention that but yet they seemed to be communicating with one another. What made me think that was they were all looking at one another and they would all pause for a moment and then one would nod its head in the negative or in the affirmative and then they would look into her tent. I was just about to crawl back underneath my covers and cry myself to sleep until sunrise when something told me to look up. I did and the last thing that I remember was seeing a gigantic set of dark, black eyes staring back at me. I opened my mouth to scream but I don't think that anything came out.

The next day all four of us woke up at the exact same time and we were all outside of our tents. Josie didn't remember anything from the night before, not even my smacking her and in fact, she was also the only one who hadn't remembered what we had seen and heard while out on the docks either. My other friends did and so did I but we were all just very confused by why we were outside of our tents and how we had gotten to be that way. We couldn't figure it out. There was no one who knew we were out there who could have been messing with us and all three of my friends were suspicious of one another, and me. I wasn't because I had full recall of the middle of the night and what I had seen. I remembered it all but was still too afraid to say anything. We had planned on staying another night but we all felt very strange, like we had been drugged and though none of us outright said it, we all felt like something terrible happened and was still going on in the woods all around us. Josie seemed to be the least concerned and asked if we wanted to go for a quick swim before we left but we all said we didn't want to. That seemed to upset her but she didn't push the issue. No one asked if we were going to explore and see where those fireball looking things had landed the night before either. Josie didn't remember it but the rest of us did. Just as we were about to leave Josie mentioned that the back of her neck was stinging and when we looked she had what looked like an old surgical scar back there. Whatever it was looked healed already and the skin was puffy and raised. We asked her how she had gotten the scar but she said she didn't have a scar there. The rest of us checked the backs of the others' necks but no one else had anything there and no one else felt any pain there either. As we made our way out to the main road, Josie talked about the strange nightmare she had the night before about strange creatures and even mentioned how I had slapped her in the dream because she was staring out into the woods. I laughed along with her but our other two friends didn't laugh. It was like something unspoken hung between us but we weren't able to put our fingers on what it was.

It would take about twenty years before we would all realize we each had a different piece of the memory from that night. We met for our usual annual lunch back in early 2007 and that's when one of us brought up that night in the woods. It turns out my other two friends had seen the beings surrounding Josie's tent as well but they didn't remember it all until years later. They also noticed they had the same type of healed wound she had suddenly woken up with as well. One of them on her right ankle and the other behind her left ear. Mine is behind my right knee. We had all noticed them the day we got home while showering but we just never thought to mention it. We haven't been hypnotically regressed yet though it's definitely on the table and we all have a feeling it somehow started with and revolves around Josie. Maybe it's just the camp and we happened to be in the wrong place at the wrong time but I doubt it. We keep in almost constant contact now and have been incessantly researching. You see, after it happened all the way until that dinner we had together in 2007, it's like we simply forgot about it. Every time I would remember, and this turned out to be true for the other three girls as well, we immediately would forget and it would be fuzzy and like it was only a dream anyway. It's very hard to explain but the more we learn, the more we hear others' encounter and abduction stories, the more we believe that's what happened to us. We believe we were abducted. We had even gone back to the camp just as regularly as we always had gone right up until we graduated high school and moved on with our lives but none of us ever gave any of it a second thought because we couldn't remember even our own conversations about it or other connections we had already made about all of it. It's still very confusing but I am sure that something happened to us that night, probably other times since then and possibly even times before that but we simply can't remember. I am terrified of learning the truth and so are my friends. Josie is the only one who doesn't seem to be as scared and she will more than likely be the first one to be regressed. I'll write about how that goes when the time comes. I have no memory of ever seeing the beings again; not in dreams, nightmares or otherwise. But I know somewhere deep down in the recesses of my mind that the memories are there because I just instinctively know that I have seen them other times. I just know it. We are planning on going back and seeing what's left of the summer camp nowadays and if we can legally camp out there for the weekend. I'll write about how that goes too, provided I leave there with my memory intact. Thanks for letting me get this all down and out there, before I forget it again. Maybe someone with a missing link or piece will come across it, who knows? After all, stranger things have happened.

CHAPTER 2
CLOAKED ENTITY STALKING MY CAMP

I was in my late twenties when I had my encounter with something I have never been able to explain but that nowadays many more people are also encountering and I don't feel so crazy about it anymore so I finally decided to write it all down. I was camping near my house in Tennessee, just me, and I had already been out there for three days when I came across something terrifying and still very unexplainable. I had chosen a spot way out in the middle of nowhere and there were so many trees and so much brush, there almost wasn't any space even for my small tent. I cleared a space though and I was having a great time. I was out there just because I had some free time and I loved hiking and being in the wilderness in general. There were no other people out there and normally there weren't any because I always went to one spot that's private property. However, my boss at the time owned it and had planned on clearing it all out and building on it but for whatever reason the permits and all the legal stuff was holding the project up. So, not only was I able to hike to my heart's content and be left alone while I was doing it, it was a win-win because in exchange for letting me camp there he expected me to keep an eye on the place and make sure there were no trespassers or vandals, things like that. I kept a shotgun on me at all times but I didn't hunt and otherwise never had to use it before. I was trained on how to use guns properly, I just never felt the need to use one before. I had just gotten back to my camp, made a fire and had something to eat. I went to bed at around eleven at night but all night long I kept hearing the sound of something large moving around in the woods directly surrounding my tent. At one point the sounds got so close it was like someone was standing right outside of my tent. I kept looking out but didn't see anything and eventually I convinced myself that it was probably a smaller animal than what it sounded like and that more than likely it was more scared of me than I was of it. I went to sleep.

The next morning I woke before sunrise and had some coffee and breakfast then went to go and explore one of my favorite trails. I didn't know the whole area yet but I was quickly becoming acquainted with most of it. It was the nineteen eighties and I had my walkman with me, complete with an array of cassette tapes for my listening pleasure and I normally had them on full blast when I would go out on my hikes. That entire day though I felt like I was being watched and normally I would have brushed that feeling off too but because of the noises the night before, I was starting to think that I wasn't alone out there after all. The day was uneventful despite the strange feelings of creepiness and terror that would wash over me seemingly randomly and for no apparent reason. It wouldn't be long before something proved my instincts to be correct but it's somewhat of a long story in getting to that. Once night fell I built a fire again and as I was sitting in my chair and eating dinner, I had the headphones off. It was just me and the sounds of nature and perfectly normal, at first. I was looking up in the sky and saw a giant flash of light like lightning but it was in the shape of an oval and it was bright orange. It almost looked like a giant ball of fire that just flashed into existence in the sky. I almost dropped my food when I saw it and stood up in order to try and get a better look. The giant ball of flame got smaller and larger several times and it seemed like it was pulsating or something. Then, just as quickly as it had appeared, it was gone and though I was a bit rattled, I considered myself a practical man and tried to forget about it. That night passed the same way as the night before, with me hearing someone or something lurking around my camp all night but once again I didn't see anything. The next day my whole life would change.

I woke up and once again just went about my usual business. There was no sign that anyone or anything had been anywhere near my camp and once again I rationalized it all. I was planning on exploring a new area of the land that day but had run out of batteries for my walkman. I couldn't find the extras I had bought and so I just went on my hike in the silence of mother nature. I noticed right away there didn't seem to be as much activity as there normally was for that time of day and once I reached a certain spot, where I believed was dead center in the middle of the forest, or at least the part of it that my boss owned, there was no noise at all. It wasn't like a slow fading of noise or anything but it was like someone had flipped a switch and not only did the whole forest fall silent all at once, but the sky was very suddenly overcast as well. There was no rain in the forecast for the whole week I had planned on being out there and I still had three more nights and four days left before I planned on or wanted to go back home. I said a silent prayer that it wouldn't rain because I hated being out camping when everything was wet and slippery. Just as I picked my bag back up and started walking towards where I thought the lake was, I heard a strange clicking sound. It was coming from two different places and seemed almost like communication of some sort. It wasn't any animal or insect that I knew of and it immediately and seemingly for no reason at all struck a terror into my soul unlike anything I had ever felt or experienced before. It sounded like it was coming from somewhere above me and as soon as I looked up, it started to rain heavily. I decided to put my backpack over my head and continue on to the water. Despite the rain being unusually heavy, especially for something that hadn't been picked up in the forecast at all, I figured it was a sun shower and would quickly pass. The clicking sounds continued the whole way to the lake. I was getting agitated. There was something about the noises that made me absolutely terrified and it blew my mind because there seemed to be no rational explanation or reason for why I was feeling that way. I kept going.

I eventually made it to the clearing where the water was and went to go and sit down near where the water met the woods, so to speak. I was determined to wait out the rain and after a while I was bored and started looking all around for the source of the now incessant clicking sounds. I didn't see anything right away. Then,

I saw something I will never forget. I looked over to where the sounds were coming from as they had moved from seemingly above me to somewhere over to my right, right on the shore near where I was sitting. I saw something that was walking on two legs, just like a human being, and that looked like a human being from the feet to the neck area, but had the head of some sort of creature. It seemed to be looking straight ahead and not at me, just from judging how the legs were moving and the swinging of the arms. At least that's what made the most sense at the time. I couldn't take my eyes off of it because it wasn't there, not really, and I was only seeing it because it was raining. It was some sort of entity that was very obviously cloaked and a movie I had recently seen in the theaters immediately came into my head. It was the predator, from the movie with the same name. I was shocked and had somehow forgotten to be terrified for a few minutes. The entity was clicking but then I heard a loud squawking noise come from behind me which not only snapped me out of my complacent daze but that also seemed to have alerted the creature to my presence. Its head quickly whipped over to look right at me. It didn't have any colors to it and was visible only because it was wet but the shape of the head was very odd. The skull seemed to be elon-gated and, as crazy as it sounds I know, it looked like it had dreadlocks for hair, on the elongated head. It looked at me and I immediately jumped up, ready to run. Then I remembered I had my gun on me and grabbed it.

The entity or whatever it was started walking towards me very quickly. I aimed the gun at it and it squawked again, this time much louder. It seemed angry and its walk showed me it was feeling aggressive towards me. I kept hearing the other one, despite not being able to see it, and that one sounded like it was also getting closer and approaching me as well, but from behind me somewhere. I took a shot at the one in front of me and it seemed to be more stunned by the noise than anything else. Here's the thing, I KNOW I hit it. The bullet seemed to go right through it though but instead of making it more angry it turned and took off at a superhuman speed into the woods. I don't know if I was in some sort of induced daze or something but I actually took off after it. It was moving so quickly though I didn't stand a chance at catching up to it and something told me it was actually going slowly to keep me able to see it. As soon as we got to the edge of the trees it scrambled up to the top of one, again at lightning fast speed. I just stood there, looking up at it. I watched as it ran incredibly fast across the tops of the trees until it was so far away I only knew it was still there because I could see the effect its weight had on the treetops. Understand though that it was in the actual tops of the tree and those branches couldn't hold a little kid's weight without snapping let alone a full grown man's or whatever this thing was. Yet, I watched it with my own eyes. I was suddenly aware of the one behind me that I had forgotten about when I started chasing the one I had taken a shot at. I turned around and saw more of them, about three or four, come walking nonchalantly and like it was nothing, right out of the water. I took off running and left everything but the gun at the water's edge.

I could hear it behind me for a little while and I didn't dare turn around. By the time I got back to my camp I was out of breath and fairly sure that it was no longer following me. However, there were at least six of them out there and those are only the ones that I had seen. It stopped raining just as suddenly as it had started and I was aware immediately that unless the sun hit them just right, I would no longer be able to see them or even know they were there if they had decided to quietly sneak up on me. I was petrified and wasn't going to stick around another second. I packed up as much of my gear as I could in a hurry and as I did so, suddenly, all of the trees started bending down towards me at the tops. They were there and they were standing

on top of the trees, surrounding me. I yelled out that I
didn't want any trouble and that I was sorry for
encroaching on their land. The tree tops bounced up
and went back to normal once I said that and I bolted
out of there as fast as I could. I left a lot of my belong-
ings behind but it didn't matter and I never went back
there again to retrieve them either. I never went back
there again, period! I tried to tell my boss about it but he
just laughed. I eventually stopped mentioning it. I
wonder if the light in the sky had anything to do with
the creatures or if they came from under the water.
Maybe the light in the sky landed in the water and those
things had gotten out somehow. I don't know what
their intentions were except that somewhere deep
down they seemed extremely evil and despite my not
really being able to see them they were downright terrifying. In the past ten years or so I see more and more
stories about these same cloaked or translucent entities
and for the most part people think they're extraterrestrial. I would like to know how the people who made
the Predator movie got it so right though. I mean, how
is that even possible? I don't know what I saw but I
never stopped searching for answers. Even if an entity
were cloaked it stands to reason to me that they could
still be shot but my bullet went right through the thing,
of that I'm sure. I wonder if there really are secret

extraterrestrial bases not only underground but underneath water sources all over the planet as well, not just in oceans like a lot of people seem to think. I've never seen them again and my boss ended up building a huge house on the land but I never went to visit and ended up quitting after not too long after my experience on his property anyway. I do wonder though if he or anyone else in his family has ever seen anything out of the ordinary or not. I might look him up and ask him if he's still alive. This wasn't my last experience with extraterrestrials either, though it was my first and it was my last with that particular entity. I am still too terrified to write about the other experiences though, but this is a good first step I think.

CHAPTER 3
OUIJA IN THE WOODS

My best friend and I went camping with my family in 1995 and we did something so incredibly stupid that has changed our lives forever and we had an experience we will never forget because of it. My parents had a very large and state of the art, for the time, camper van that they had just bought and they wanted to take it into the woods to camp for one of our vacations that year. I was eleven years old and didn't want to go without my best friend Gina. Gina lived next door and our moms had been pregnant with us at the same time and were also best friends. Of course our parents were okay with her coming with us and off we went for our end of summer vacation in the woods. There was an area near our home, about an hour's drive away, where you could bring your camper into the woods and park it for your stay. There was also a place for people who wanted to camp out the old fashioned way in tents and stuff but the areas were just a little bit separate from one another. While we had our own spot where the van was parked and where we could barbecue and build our own fire, there were other people around and it wasn't like we were all alone out there in the deep dark woods. It was a National Park, I don't want to say the name of it and somewhere we had gone so many times before. We knew we would have fun and this was Gina's first time ever camping which made me even more excited about the whole thing. I was like a kid on the night before Christmas and Gina was really excited too. We made it to the park and found our spot. We went to work making food and building a campfire.

Though the camper was very modern and a little fancy, it wasn't brand new. While my parents went to work outside of the van, me and Gina hung out inside and started planning all of the things we wanted to do while we were there. We were hungry and waiting for my parents to get dinner ready. We were looking through the cabinets for something to snack on to hold us over when we found a Ouija board. We both loved horror movies and had been watching them for years at that point and though we hadn't ever seen or handled one in real life, we had seen the board in movies and thought we knew what it was and what it did. Needless to say we had no idea and I wish we hadn't ever found that board. But, we did find it and we were excited about it. My parents were religious but they weren't fanatics or anything. However, I knew my mother would blow a gasket if she knew there had been a Ouija board in the van when they bought it and not only that but that me and my friend planned on using it. We hid the board and decided we would wait until we were able to go into the woods and do something by ourselves to use it so my parents didn't see it. If we had to, we figured we would just leave it there in the woods and forget about it. We were dying to try it though and were excited by the alleged danger using it brought with it. Finally dinner was ready and we went outside to hang out with my parents. We knew there was a place to go swimming and so we asked my parents if we could go there the next day. They said that they had wanted to do some hiking to the other side of the park but that if we promised to stay together and if we agreed to take the map, that we could go swimming without them the following morning. After all, it stood to reason that we wouldn't be alone and even that there would be other kids there too because the place had looked very busy when we pulled in and paid for some park extras at the welcome station. It was the nineties and things were very different back then than they are nowadays.

The first night there was really fun and my parents even joined in when we told spooky and creepy stories by the campfire. The van slept four people which was perfect because me and Gina always shared a bed at sleepovers anyway. We stayed in the back of the van and my parents pulled their bed out of a wall in the front of it, right behind the driver and passenger seats. The next morning we woke up bright and early and my dad already had breakfast almost done. Gina and I put on our swimsuits, we put our clothes on over them and then we packed our backpacks with snacks, drinks and other things we wanted to bring swimming with us. I put the Ouija board and planchette in my bag and we left after a very long and boring lecture from my parents about staying together in the woods, the areas where we could get help, reading and following the map and what we would call today "stranger danger." We hiked through the woods and though we passed maybe one or two elderly couples, we didn't see as many people as we expected along the way. We didn't think anything of that and kept going. Finally, we made it to the swimming spot but we were surprised that there were only about ten other people there and no other kids. There were no little kids and no kids our age. There were no older teenagers either and in fact we noticed that there were only old people, which to our eleven year old selves consisted of anyone over the age of thirty.

We thought it was weird but it didn't concern us or anything. We knew we had to be back to the van for dinner, which was going to be at seven o'clock and we brought our lunches with us. We swam and played for a while and after we ate our lunch and a few hours had passed, we decided to try out the Ouija board. I didn't notice it at the time but looking back on it it's like as soon as we made that decision, for one reason or another every single person vacated the swimming area and Gina and I were all by ourselves. It was a bright and sunny day, despite it being almost fall, and we dried off fairly quickly in the sun. We remembered seeing people use one of the boards in a movie we had seen a few times and we just decided to do it like we remembered. We went to one of the tables in the little picnic and park area near where we had just gone swimming and placed our hands on the planchette. We giggled nervously and asked if anyone was there. In an instant the planchette moved to yes. We both had agreed beforehand that no matter what we weren't going to move it and we trusted each other so we were both shocked with how easy it had been to get an answer. Gina asked who was there with us and the word demon was spelled back to us. We both took our hands off the board immediately because, despite it being broad daylight and the fact that we were in a safe place, it scared us. We were little kids and it scared us enough that we quit right there on the spot, both of us pretending that we didn't want to stop except to please the other one and we both promised one another we would try again later on. We didn't say goodbye or thank the board or anything. We simply put it back in my book bag and went on with our day.

We had originally decided to swim some more but the day turned overcast rather quickly and we both had the distinct feeling that we were being watched. Because there was no one else around us anymore it was a scary feeling and we both knew that whatever was watching us had to have been doing so from some-where in the woods. We played a few games of cards but eventually the feeling became too much and we decided to go back to our camp earlier than we were going to at first. We made our way through the woods but it seemed like all at once everything was different. We didn't see any of the signs we had noticed coming in and couldn't find where we were on the map my parents had given us. We both knew how to read maps fairly well and yet, somehow, we got lost anyway. We weren't too concerned at first because we figured we would eventually come across someone who would be able to help us but after what seemed like forever but was really about an hour of walking and not seeing anyone, we became not only very worried but we were also pretty exhausted as well. We sat on a large tree stump waiting for someone to walk by but no one did and to take our minds off what was going on we once again decided to pull the Ouija board out. We placed it on the ground and knelt in front of it. After saying hello we once again asked who was there and we got the response "death." That was it and we were so frazzled by that point that I took the board and tossed it into the woods along with the planchette. Gina and I knew it would be dark soon and we were definitely not equipped to be out there in the middle of the wilderness, alone, at night time. We just kept right on walking in the direction of where we believed our camp was, hoping we would just run into it somehow, eventually.

It was dark out and we were still lost. We were both crying by that time and still hadn't seen a single sign or other living soul the whole time. It was eerie because we knew that we should have seen several of both of those things. Finally we stopped to rest again and that's when an old man seemed to come out of nowhere, and asked us if we were lost. We were crying but so thankful to see him we both jumped and told him that yes we were lost and we needed help. He smiled but when he did it was terrifying. His smile didn't reach his eyes and his teeth were broken and stained by what looked like tobacco. We were good kids and didn't want to be rude so we suppressed our initial fear and gut instincts and told the man where we needed to go. He was really thin and looked like your average old man. He was a bit hunched in the back, had very thin, white hair and his skin was very pale and full of liver spots. He told us he knew right where that was, where we told him our camper was, and he told us to follow him. He whistled a tune as he walked and it was creepy. I don't know how else to describe it. The man had a flashlight he handed to me and though he was leading the way and the forest was pitch black, he didn't seem to need one. He was also dressed very oddly for where we were because he was wearing what looked like a tailor made three piece suit and very shiny shoes. His cane looked like a big snake and was perfectly carved by hand. Gina and I just looked at each other and after fifteen minutes of walking we realized we didn't know this old man and that we could be putting ourselves in even more harm's way than we were before we met him. He could be a psycho for all we knew. We didn't say anything though in case he was helping us we didn't want to be rude to him. We both were still crying and we were both extremely scared.

Eventually he turned to us and I will never forget the look on his face. It was evil and his whole appearance had somehow been transformed. He wasn't a kindly old man anymore but a grotesque thing that neither me nor Gina knew how to classify. The old man was still there, we could still see him, but we also knew there was something else underneath. We both screamed. He told us to shut up and knew both of our names despite us knowing for sure we hadn't given it to him. He told us to stay put and we did as we were told and sat on a log there in the middle of the forest. There still hadn't been anyone around and within a minute the old man returned. He looked even more devilish at that point and it was almost like the facade of the old man was slowly fading away and the evil underneath was seeping through more and more. He pulled the Ouija board out from behind his back and said we had been bad girls for throwing it the way we had. He pointed to me. "You!" he said, and his voice was almost a growl at that point, "come here." I didn't move and started screaming. His eyes were flames in his head and weren't kind and bright blue anymore. By that time Gina was screaming with me and he told us both to shut up. Suddenly he was standing straight up and had to have been about nine feet tall. His body contorted and turned into a half man, half goat looking thing as we looked on in terror. "Use the board" he demanded. We both shook our heads no and started screaming again. Then, coming from out of the darkness I heard my father's voice calling mine and Gina's names. I must have passed out and I guess Gina did too.

I woke up lying next to Gina on our bed in the camper. I immediately called for my dad and Gina grabbed my hand. We were both too weak to do anything other than lay there but we were also both absolutely terrified of what we had been through. My dad came running into the van while my mom spoke to the park rangers outside. I looked up at my dad and he smiled and told me it would all be okay. However, standing right behind him but too blurry almost for me to be able to see, was the old man. He wasn't in the old man form but the top of his body was that of a very physically fit god and the bottom that of a goat. He still held his snake cane but then he pointed it at me and Gina and started to laugh the most evil laugh I had ever heard. I started crying and sobbing and Gina must've seen him too because she was also shaking like crazy and sobbing. My dad tried to comfort us but the devil stood behind him the whole time, mocking him. We went back to sleep and didn't wake up until breakfast the next morning. My parents looked at us, concerned but asked us anyway what happened the day before. We told them everything except for the part where we played with the Ouija board and the part where the old man transformed into a devil. We knew they wouldn't believe us anyway. They told us the rangers said no one fitting that description, as far as they knew, had been in the park at that time. They also asked us why we had ignored all the people we passed along the way while we were lost who had asked if we were okay and offered to help us. That really confused us because we hadn't seen another living soul the whole time we were wandering around out there. Gina and I just looked at each other and my parents must've seen how it was upsetting us, though they couldn't have possibly guessed how much or why, and thankfully, they dropped the subject.

We weren't allowed to go off on our own anymore for the rest of the trip but that was okay with us because we really didn't want to. We never saw that Ouija board again but that old man/devil beast haunted our dreams and even visited us sometimes while we were wide awake, usually in the middle of the night and when we were together, many times after that. Finally when we were sixteen we came across some information that said if we got a Ouija board and properly closed it, by saying goodbye, it would be the end of the whole ordeal. We did it and it was but I still wonder what it was we were really dealing with that day and if it/he is ever going to come back for us. I know it's a lot and some-what hard to believe but I implore you, please don't ever mess with something like an Ouija board or other divining tools unless you know what you're doing. As an adult I've searched for answers and have come to the conclusion based on my research that we hadn't encountered a devil that day but some sort of forest demon that feeds off of fear, especially the fear of chil-dren. I think we woke whatever it was up with the board and though I haven't gone back there since then to see for sure, I think it's probably still roaming around out there preying on people. It makes sense because that particular national park is known for bizarre events and people mysteriously dying and disappearing and while that's always been the case with that place in particular but also for places like it all over the world, there seemed to have been a huge uptick in cases since the mid nineties when me and Gina used the board. We must've opened a portal or something. I am going back there next summer and I am going to bring my own

Ouija board, now that I know how to use it, and see if I can somehow close whatever portal or vortex we opened. While I know we aren't responsible for most of what happens there, I can't help but feel a little guilty because I do believe we played a role at least in some part of it. Thanks for letting me share this.

CHAPTER 4
THE TALL DEMON

When I was twenty-six years old back in 2012 I had an encounter that terrified me and that also changed my life. I still have nightmares about it and despite having done as much research as I possibly could to figure out what it was and why it happened to me, I still really don't have any answers. I decided to use my vacation time to go and visit my parent's cabin in Colorado. They bought it when I was a little girl and I have so many fond memories of going there as a family and with all of our family, ever since. It was the middle of winter and I was going through a lot in my life and needed to get away. I hadn't ever asked to go by myself before but my parents weren't concerned at all with giving me the key and they handed it right over. We live in Pennsylvania but my older sister lived in Colorado at the time with her family and she still does. She said she would stop by and spend a night with me while I was there. I was planning on staying for a whole week.

There was a ton of snow on the ground by the time I got to the cabin. It was one of those places like you always see in horror movies. It was desolate, way out in the middle of nowhere and there were no neighbors. I should mention that I had always had nightmares when we stayed there but that wasn't anything completely new and I was always very sensitive to things around us at all times that other people can't see and aren't aware of. I thought about that on the drive to the place from the airport. I had always had bad dreams and visions, sometimes even when I was wide awake and it was dark in my bedroom, of a strange looking, tall man who would either come from under the bed or out of the closet and just stand at the foot of the bed watching me while I laid there. I got the chills but decided that it was all little kid's stuff and I wasn't going to allow it to ruin my sanctuary for the week. I really needed to get away and just go off grid for a while and that's exactly what I intended to do. I was even initially reluctant to have to visit with my sister, despite not having seen her for almost five years. We didn't have a falling out or anything. It's just she was busy with work and her family and I had a full time job where it felt like I never got any time to myself to do anything other than work. As far as the cabin, my uncle- my mother's brother- had a run of bad luck and had been staying there for the last ten years and so other than to visit him we didn't go there. We stopped being able to vacation there once he moved in because he was a weirdo and a drunk and though she helped him the moment he came to her and expressed he needed somewhere to live, he and my mother weren't that close because of his erratic and sometimes violent, drunken behavior. I knew my uncle wouldn't be there though because he had died six months earlier and my sister had just gotten done cleaning out all of his possessions and having the place professionally cleaned. So, that's the back story, now let's get into my encounter.

I pulled off the access road and almost didn't make it to where I had to put my car because of all of the snow. It didn't matter to me because I had hiked in the snow before, admittedly never while there was this much still falling and on the ground, but I wasn't worried. The cabin wasn't like a house where you pull up and into a driveway or anything. It was in the middle of the woods and it was going to be quite a hike to get there. Once I saw what the weather was like I knew that my sister wasn't going to be coming to visit until possibly the end of the week or at the very least for a couple of days. I was going to end up snowed in and in the middle of the woods. I relished the thought. It was hard living, being in the cabin. The bathroom was in the woods and the electricity came from a little generator. It was almost like camping in a camper van but it was bigger. I finally made it to the cabin with almost no time to spare before night fell. I was lucky because I don't know how I would have made it through the snow and the woods to continue on or to turn back in the dark. I didn't plan the hike out there very well. My sister had stocked the place with food but all I wanted was a hot shower and some sleep. I took a shower and settled in my bedroom. Before I was able to go to sleep though I realized I had forgotten to turn off the generator for the night. I reluctantly put on my jacket and sneakers, grabbed my flashlight and went to head out the front door. I stopped short before I got to it though because as I walked up to it it was turning. Someone was trying to get in. Now, my rational mind knew that it was impossible because nobody lived out there and my parents owned miles of land as far as the eye could see so even if someone were dumb enough to have been camping out there at the time, they would have seen the private property signs. Still, I thought that maybe it was someone who was out there and hadn't known it was going to snow and was now seeking shelter. I'm sorry but I wasn't their girl. I never had a good deed done for a stranger go unpunished and plus I was all alone out there. Unless it was a young woman or a child, there was no chance anyone was obtaining shelter through me, that was for sure. I asked who was there but there was no answer. I walked over to the door and stared out the peephole but there was no one there. As soon as I looked through it, the knob stopped jiggling and turning. I took a deep breath and opened the door. All I needed to do was walk to the back of the cabin, turn off the generator and run back through the front door and into my room. I stopped immediately in my tracks though because mine weren't the only ones out there.

The other tracks weren't human though, and they looked like hooves instead of any sort of known animal in the area or another human being's. I was terrified but knew that I would never get any sleep and had to at the very least go and turn the generator off. I didn't have too much extra fuel and didn't know when the roads would be accessible again. I followed the hoof prints all the way around the cabin and to the back but they didn't lead to the generator, they led into the woods. The cabin was placed in a spot where hikers would have set up tents if the cabin hadn't been there. It was in the middle of some very deep and very dense woods. I took a deep breath and decided I needed to find out what sort of animal had been trying to get in. I reluctantly followed the tracks into the woods. I knew it was dangerous but I was going through a lot at the time and was tired of feeling like everyone's victim. I was going to face and confront the fear of the entity that had always tormented me in the bedroom of that cabin for once and for all. I walked for about five minutes before suddenly the forest went silent. The moon and stars that had just been in the sky were covered by dark gray clouds and everything got that much darker. I had a flashlight with me but it wasn't much help if I'm being honest. I stopped when the hoof prints stopped, after I had been walking in the freezing snow and cold, deeper into the woods, for about ten minutes. I shined my flashlight all around but didn't see or hear anything at first. Then, I heard someone whispering my name from behind a nearby tree. I yelled out and asked who was there. That's when the tall man stepped out from behind the tree and smiled at me.

He looked exactly like I had remembered him. He was at least ten feet tall, had large ears and an equally large, crooked nose. His skin was a pale green color, it could almost be mistaken for white if you didn't know better. Almost like something that glows in the dark looks in the light. His teeth were brown and jagged and he wore a long black duster jacket that went down to his ankles. He had on an all black suit, shiny black shoes and his eyes were blacker than anything I had ever seen before. His hair was gray and hung down to his shoulders and he wore an old, beat up looking black cowboy hat on top of his head. He said my name again but before I could respond he opened his duster. Four little creatures seemed to come right out of the lining of his jacket and the only way that I can describe them is that they looked like miniature hell demons. I started to slowly back away. His eyes flashed and suddenly they were burning red and hot like the flames of a fire. The little minions danced around him and excitedly jabbered away in some gibberish language I couldn't understand. I asked him what he wanted but he just laughed and laughed. Then, he started to come towards me. I turned and ran as fast as I could back to the cabin.

I knew he was following behind me despite my not being able to hear anything. I ran inside and locked the door and heard the little demons jabbering away in their unknown language while the doorknob jiggled and someone, I'm pretty sure I knew who it was even though I didn't dare look through the peephole again, was banging on the door. He screamed for me to let him in and his voice was more of a growl than anything else. In the past, when he had approached my bed, his voice had been even and smooth but he sounded enraged just then. I was terrified he would kick the door down at any minute. I had shut off the generator so I only had my flashlight. I started barricading the door with furniture and once I was satisfied he wouldn't get in, I went and locked myself in my bedroom. I hid under my covers like a terrified little kid and eventually the banging stopped. I looked out my bedroom window in the middle of the night because I couldn't sleep and saw that the hoof prints were no longer there and had been covered up by a fresh blanket of snow. I was starting to think that maybe I had lost my mind. I began to pray. Just as I did so it sounded like someone was stomping on the roof. It sounded like what you imagine reindeer on the roof sound like when listening for Santa at Christmas time or something and then there were four lighter sets of footprints that also seemed to be jumping up and down, stomping and stamping. I continued to pray and after two minutes or so I heard what sounded like an animal howling. I looked up and saw an incredibly bright flash of light in the sky and everything was suddenly quiet again. I must have passed out because I didn't open my eyes again until it was morning.

I immediately got up and looked out the window but there was nothing there. I went and moved every-thing away from the front door, opened it and looked outside to see if any footprints were left. There were hoof prints all over the porch. The tall man had taken his animal form when he was trying to get into the cabin. It hadn't all been some sort of terrible nightmare and despite the fact that I had known that all along, it terrified me even more nonetheless. The snow had let up and so I figured I had one more night before I was able to hike back out of there and go to where I had service to call my sister and see when she was coming. I no longer felt safe there all alone and my peace of mind had been shattered once again. I was a nervous wreck and constantly looking over my shoulder at every little noise that whole day but once nothing happened and it was nighttime again I began to relax, just a little bit. I decided to leave the generator on and let it run out in the middle of the night because there was no way I was going back outside or anywhere near those woods at night time. Not ever again. I went and read by the light coming in from the full moon and my flashlight, tucked up nice and comfortable in my bed. My comfort didn't last long.

That whole night I was woken up over and over again to sounds on the roof alternating with someone tapping on the bedroom window. No words were ever spoken except the whispering of my name and it was so low as to make it so it almost seemed like it was nothing but the wind blowing. I knew better though. The next morning I woke up to my sister knocking on the door but at first I thought it was the tall demon man and didn't answer her. I went and stared at the door and it wasn't until I saw her in the peephole that I finally opened the door. She came in and had brought breakfast. I immediately began to tell her what I was experiencing and she reluctantly told me that not only had she experienced that same entity, every time we had visited here when we were growing up, but also that towards the end of his life my uncle had been ranting and raving about miniature demons under his bed and a devil man in his closet. No one believed him, his track record for insanity was too long and distinguished by that time. We both sat in silence for a few minutes trying to comprehend that what we had each individually experienced, the entity and his minions who had so thoroughly terrified us and whom we both were starting to begin we had simply imagined, was a real being. We decided I would spend the rest of my vacation week at her house with her family. I didn't want to be alone anymore anyway. I never went back to that cabin and neither did my sister. My family sold it in 2018 and lately, mainly because I had been having nightmares about the tall demon and the little devils again, I was wondering if I should go there and see if the new owners had experienced anything like what my sister, my uncle and I all had.

I don't know what it all means but I do know that the tall man was the devil or at least a devil and that he had come for my soul. He didn't get it that time but that doesn't mean he won't keep trying. I've since gone back to church and have become stronger in my faith so maybe that's why he has been visiting me again. I don't know if it would have been anyone who was staying in that cabin or if it was just our family and I don't know what the reason was. Maybe he and the little ones feed on human being's fear. Maybe I will never know. I know a lot of people will think I'm a lunatic but I'm not looking for validation and not trying to force people to believe. I wrote this all down in case someone else has experienced that man or his minions and to let them know that they aren't alone and they have to remain strong. Otherwise, they could lose something even more precious than their minds, in that, the devil is normally only interested in your immortal soul. Thanks for letting me share and though the story isn't over yet because I haven't really learned anything new or gained any answers to my many questions, I feel like someone needed to read this anyway.

CHAPTER 5
I'LL NEVER FORGET IT

I didn't really know much about Sasquatch growing up. I remember seeing the Patterson-Gimlin film and hearing the term Bigfoot a few times but that was the extent of my knowledge, but that would all change.

My father was in the Army and after moving all over the world, we ended up in Ft. Lewis Washington. I always loved the woods, so living in the Pacific Northwest was heavenly. My friends and I would go out and hike different areas, and explore wherever we could.

In retrospect, there were many incidents at the time which seemed inconsequential, but now I know weren't. Things such as rock throwing, wood knocking, hearing strange vocalizations, and one time seeing two dark figures seemingly walking across a meadow but the distance was fairly great so I thought nothing of it.

In the fall of 1989, just after my 16th birthday, my friend and I decided to check out the area around Lewis Lake. The day was fairly uninteresting, a few critters but nothing spectacular. We were heading southwest on some trails which lead towards the river. The trail was maybe nine feet wide, pretty wooded on the left and a sparsely wooded incline leading to a tree line on the right. We were joking and cutting up when I caught a scent of something awful. The odor was a very musky stench of sulfur and wet dog mixed with the local land waste. We heard a loud snap as if a tree branch was being broken. Very soon after about forty feet in front of us to the left, we saw a massive dark brown figure step onto the trail. We both froze. With one step it was in the middle of the trail, and my mind could not make sense of what this was.

I can remember it as clear as the day it happened. This was a very large creature, eight to nine feet tall. Its body was massive and must have weighed six hundred or more pounds. It turned to look at us, but it turned from the waist not the neck. It was completely hair covered except for the face area from the brow area to below the lower lip. The facial area was a grayish color skin. The body was long with thick brown hair of different shades, and various lengths covering it. The face looked somewhat human, with a bit of a broader nose, and a wider mouth, and thick brow ridge. It had large eyes but I could not see any distinct color other than black. The shoulders were very broad and the head seemed to sit on the shoulders. The arms were muscular and seemed a bit longer then ours, not quite to the knees but very close. It had very distinct and visible fingers. The legs were very thick and muscular. This thing just looked powerful and it was very intimidating to say the least. However, it never made any type of aggressive movement or gesture.

It let out a grunt or maybe it was a heavy sigh or an audible sound of disgust. I don't know why I think that, but I did then and still do today. Was it disgusted by us or because we were there? I don't know.

It looked at us for a few seconds then turned took one more step and had crossed the trail. It snapped a few branches as it walked up the hill on the right with ease occasionally grabbing trees to pull itself up the steep incline. We stood and watched without saying a word to the other, we were definitely in shock. When it crested the top of the hill it disappeared over without ever making a glance back towards us. It clearly wasn't concerned or thought we were a threat. How could it? We were tiny compared to it. Once it disappeared my friend and I looked at one another, and without saying a word we took off running towards home. We never discussed it with anyone except for our parents who thought we'd seen a bear. I didn't get into with my parents for not believing me, heck; I still have to wonder if what I saw was real as it all just seems like a fairy tale. Only being 16 and wanting to fit in at school, I didn't utter a word nor did my friend. If our parents didn't believe us, other friends clearly wouldn't, in fact they'd probably ridicule us.

I can say that while the encounter was eye opening, I wasn't too scared to go back in the woods. I know some people get so freaked out they never venture back in, but I don't think this thing has any intention on hurting people. This isn't to say it wouldn't, but I think it only would if it were provoked.

I've never seen anything since but I have heard odd things now and then.

CHAPTER 6
NEW YORK BIGFOOT

Back in the late 1980s, my parents purchased an old farmhouse in Upstate New York in the Adirondack Mountains. The house was built in 1880 and sat on seven acres of mostly wooded land.

The farmhouse was in dire need of repair when they purchased it, but over the years they fixed it up into a very comfortable weekend and summer retreat from the urban bustle of the New York City area life we lived Monday through Friday. It took us about three and a half hours normally to get there on a Friday night, but only about three hours to return on Sunday night. I didn't mind the trip as I liked to relax and listen to music as my dad drove talking with my mom about work and other related topics a teen would find boring.

One night, after we arrived at approximately nine,

my sister and I sat at the kitchen table eating sandwiches for dinner while my parents had cocktails in the front living room. The kitchen was at the rear of the house and the windows faced a drop-off in the property which ran down to a stream which ran year round. As I ate, my Walkman playing whatever I listened to back then, I found myself gazing out the window. My sister said something to me, I answered her and went back to staring, but this time there was something in the window which was about twelve feet from the table. There, illuminated from the light spilling out of the kitchen, was a huge, ape-like face staring back at me. It had a broad, wide face, with no discernible neck and shoulders that spread out beyond the four foot wide window. The brow of the creature was heavy and I do not recall any expression on the creature's face. It was clearly and most obviously a Bigfoot, but what was different from any description that I had heard before about a Bigfoot was that the hair of this creature was more orange-like, not brown or black.

At first I was frozen, then after the initial shock wore off, I jumped up and yelled. I motioned to the window, but by the time my sister looked it was gone. My parents came rushing in, concerned for me. I frantically told them what I'd seen. My dad, who prided himself on being an action guy, grabbed a flashlight, his revolver and headed out.

My mother protested this move as she would have rather he called the sheriff, which would have easily taken upwards of an hour for them to respond. Not listening to my mom, my dad raced outside.

From the window where I'd see the face, we watch as my dad's flashlight darted back and forth in the yard, then the woods. He was out there for about ten minutes then came in.

He said he didn't see anything and sat me down. With a stern look he asked if I was telling the truth. I swore I was. He then said it would be impossible for a person to be looking in the window as it was eight feet off the ground and he didn't see anything out there for anyone to stand on.

I swore that I had seen what I'd seen. He trusted me and told my mom to make sure all the doors were locked that night.

I went to bed, the face on my mind the entire time. The window to my bedroom faced the back and was the same height off the ground as the kitchen. I didn't want something staring at me so I closed the blinds.

I never saw anything ever again and my dad never asked me about it after that night. I know what I saw. It was a creature and it had orangey hair like an orangutan, but with the face of a Bigfoot. I've since looked up many an encounter in the Adirondack area and know without a doubt what I'd seen. My parents sold the cabin my first year in college, otherwise I would have gone back to search for the creature.

CHAPTER 7

MONKEY BOY

The year was the late summer of 1998 in the Upper Peninsula of Michigan. There was a lake nearby where my brother and I would go canoeing a lot. (I don't want to say specifically where, sorry, but I don't want a bunch of Bigfoot researcher wannabes converging on my town.) As we paddled down a small stretch in the water, we came into an area where enormous boulders and covered each side of the bank. That's when something caught my eye about forty yards away on the bank to my left. At first I thought it was a boy, but something was off as this 'boy' looked like it was covered in hair. It wasn't wearing clothes, but instead had light brown fur covering its body. It was also very lean, not muscular like other people's description of Bigfoot are, in fact, I'm not sure that what's this was. Maybe it's a juvenile, but whatever it was, it looked like a monkey that walked on two legs.

As I watched it, it appeared to not notice us as it was staring off down the river, looking away from us. My brother immediately stopped talking, this told me he had now seen it too. We sat there floating and watching this thing wondering just what on God's green Earth we were seeing. I wished now I had a camera, but like everyone else's encounter stories, they either don't have one (that's me), or they don't take it out to use and then there's the occasional blurry picture.

Suddenly, the creature, or whatever it was, turned its head and looked directly at us, as if it had known we were watching it all along. This sent chills down my spine. The features on this thing wasn't like other descriptions of a Bigfoot. It had enormous yellow eyes — the biggest eyes I've ever seen on a mammal ever, it kind of looked cartoonish. The nose was shaped like what you'd see on a lemur and the thing had a scary grin stretched across its hairy face. I do need to disclose that the sun was setting, so the angle of light could have made it appear like it had a grinning face. Either way, it was creepy and we both were scared.

The creature stood about five feet and like I mentioned above it was lean, skinny really. It stared at us, and us at it. I'll admit that while its grin was off putting, I wasn't really scared nor was my brother. We were both mesmerized by the thing and it appeared to be so with us. I don't know how long we all watched the other, but it felt like it was five minutes.

The creature then turned away from us and disappeared into the woods. I gave my brother a puzzled look and said, "What in the hell was that?"

He replied, "I have no idea."

With dusk fast approaching, we turned the canoe around and headed back. The entire time we talked about our encounter. We guessed with was some sort of Bigfoot. I didn't know they came in varieties, but his was not, I repeat, was not your typical Patty looking creature and I feel confident saying it was a juvenile Bigfoot either. That only leaves it to be some sort of rarer cryptid.

We arrived back at the place we put in and got out. The sun was down and we had maybe ten more minutes of light left. We both hurried up, more out of an abundance of fear for we didn't want to be out there. If it was a juvenile of some rare cryptid, I didn't momma to coming looking for us.

We didn't tell many people about our experience. I think it's safe to say most people don't believe and those that do will probably not believe we saw a rare type of cryptid. It's like you can't win with this sighting.

We visited the lake often afterwards, but never saw it again and we never had the courage to go to the exact spot and look for it. No sense tempting fate.

CHAPTER 8
HOG EATER

I was hog hunting from a tree stand in east Texas back in the early 90s. My day had started early like usual, around 5am. As normal I put out sliced apples and table scraps to hold the hogs for a few minutes for a shot. I got in my tree stand and waited for the woods to settle down and the sun to rise.

At sunup, I heard hogs rooting around, working the river's edge, which was about forty yards away. The hogs were coming towards me. I could first see them to my left at about 45 degrees, about thirty yards out, but I still didn't have a clear shot.

I waited for them to close in on the bait I had left where I'd have a clear and clean shot. It was then I noticed movement to my right about seventy yards out. I put my scope on it but could only make out what appeared to be the side of someone's face. Keep in mind it was still a bit dark out as the sun was just rising. I blinked heavily and looked again to notice it was covered in hair and was moving slowly through the woods towards the hogs as if it was stalking them.

The thing stopped at a tree and peered around it in the direction of the hogs which were still moving towards me. It then moved from around the tree towards another, it did this several times in a leap frog type maneuver until it was about ten yards away from the unsuspecting hogs.

I could see most of its body, it was huge, standing on two legs, and like I mentioned before, it was covered in thick hair.

I was beginning to get scared. What exactly was I looking at? I had heard of Bigfoot or Boogers, as I've heard them called in east Texas and other parts of the south. However, I always dismissed people's stories as fantasies or outright lies told for attention.

But here I was looking at one. It was yards away and still it hadn't noticed me, and I was praying it wouldn't.

The hogs reached my bait and began to eat. With their attention on the bait, the creature made its move. It came from around the tree it had been using for cover, cleared the distant in a few strides and snatched one of the hogs. The other hogs took off squealing. The hog it had in its grasp squealed and squired frantically. The creature had it by a hind leg. It swung up and slammed the hog into the ground. The hog was still alive. It did it once more, this time killing it.

I was petrified. I know how large a hog is and this thing made it look like a small pot belly pig if that helps with scale. My index finger had made it to the trigger of my rifle and I now had the scope fixed dead center on the creature.

With the dead hog in its grasp, he brought it up and with ease ripped off a leg and began to eat. It was then I thought I was going to faint. I must have made a movement because it stopped eating and looked right at me.

I was frozen with fear. To this day I don't know how I didn't piss or shit my pants. It leered at me and grimaced with its bloody mouth. This things eyes were black as coal and it looked angry. I was mere yards from it and the temptation to shoot it was in me, but I was also afraid. What if I shot it and missed? Not something I was known for, but what if? Or what if I hit it and my round wasn't enough to take this thing down. It was big, and if I were to guess it had to weigh around four hundred pounds and was easily eight feet tall. Its shoulders were wide and muscular, hell; it was ripped. It could tear my limb off as easy as it had done it to the hog.

I lowered my rifle and raised my left hand in a vain attempt to give a single of truce.

It grimaced again and let out a low guttural growl. It then turned, hog still in its grasp and raced off. With about six long strides it was gone.

I relaxed into my tree stand, my body trembling. I was in shock, there was no doubt. I had come face to face, almost literally with a creature I thought up until minutes before was a joke.

After calming myself down, I got out of the tree stand and headed back to my car. I was done hunting for the day and for the remaining hog season.

I have since gone hunting but I've never seen the creature again. I'm not sure if I want to either as once in my life is enough.

CHAPTER 9
NIGHT VISITORS

What I'm about to detail occurred in the early 1990s when I lived near the Tetons in eastern Idaho.

I worked as an electrical contractor and had been contracted to do the electrical for a large house being built in the foothills. I was busy that summer but also know how this work can be feast or famine so I took it even though I had two other jobs I was working on. I also happened to be recently single and dove into my work.

With the job promising to pay a decent amount I chose to work over the weekend. It would give me something to do during a time I normally would have been with my ex and working on a job site alone was kind of nice. The peace and quiet along with the sounds of nature just outside promised to make for a fun weekend.

To make matters more enjoyable I got permission to park my 5th wheel on site so I could work from sunrise to sundown or longer and not have to drive the forty minutes back and forth.

After my first day I was tired. I had gotten a lot done and only needed Sunday to finish up. I was really excited.

I made a nice fire in what would eventually be their front yard and set up a table and chair so I could relax and prepare my dinner. I had brought a tri-tip which I had marinated and my mouth was watering just at the thought of diving into it.

With the fire roaring now and the meat cooking, I cracked open an ice cold beer and relaxed into the chair to enjoy the last bits of light. The days were long in Idaho during the summer, with us being close to the edge of the time zones and up north, it didn't get dark until almost 10pm. While many would enjoy this fact, just imagine the winters, yep you guessed it, very short days.

During this time I had also gotten into journaling and while I waited for the tri-tip to cook, I opened my journal and began to write about my day, my thoughts, and even my visions for my future. You see I was single like I said, but my breakup with my ex had really hurt me. I had taken to journaling to deal with the process and I can attest it works.

I was about to finish putting a period on the last sentence when I heard a rock hit close by. I looked up and saw the rock specifically. It was a chunk of granite about the size of a golf ball. I looked around and knew it just didn't fall from the sky. This meant someone was in the woods.

Not afraid, I called out. "Hey who's there? No messing around, okay. Come on out and enjoy some amazing tri-tip and a cold beer."

No response. Not that I expected one.

I then heard some rustling in the treelined about thirty feet away.

Now would be a good time to detail the building site. The house was being constructed on the edge of the forest, the front of the house had a view of the valley and beyond east, and the back of the house was tucked into the woods, and backed up to the foothills which eventually led up the towering peaks of the Teton Mountains.

This meant the rock came from near the back of the house.

I called out again, "Hey, just come out and say hello. I promise I won't bite."

No response to my call. The rustling stopped each time I called out. This told me whoever it was heard me.

"Fine, leave it all to me," I joked. I put my journal down and checked on the meat. It was cooked perfectly. I removed it from the flame and set it on the table wrapped in aluminum foil so it could rest.

I sat back down and was greeted with another rock. It landed close by the first one.

I laughed and took a swig of beer. I really didn't think much of it, just thought it was probably some teenagers acting fools, much like I had when I was a teen.

I continued to hear rustling and what clearly sounded like light footfalls for the next hour as I ate my tri-tip and potatoes. I thought if they wanted to mess around, go ahead, I wasn't going to have them disturb my meal.

I finished up. Tossed the trash into a bag and decided to go inside and look around, I hoped to coordinate the next days work.

Once inside, lantern in hand, I did all I needed to so that I'd be ready to hit the ground running in the morning.

I opened the front door to see someone running away with the trash bag. I called out for them to stop as at first I didn't know what they had taken. I ran after them, stopping at the treeline. I called out for them to stop this time and that I meant it. By the way, I did mean it. I was and still am a nice guy, but don't push me around.

I went back to find large tracks around the fire, my gear, and the chair. I knelt and examined the prints, these were huge, like fourteen inches long and six to seven inches wide. I could clearly see toes meaning these were prints of a bare foot.

I suddenly had a tinge of fear hit me. Was this a Bigfoot? I wondered to myself. Was I really visited by a creature that only tin-foil hatted conspiracy people believed in?

I wanted to deny it, but I was looking at the large prints and what I saw running away, while not completely clear, looked big and dark. A bit spooked. I got my gear, cooler, and my sleeping bag and decided I'd sleep inside the house instead of my truck.

Inside I did my best to secure the doors and placed my stuff upstairs on the second floor in a bedroom which had a view of my truck. It wasn't really too dark out as there was a moon about three quarters providing a lot of light. Those who live in the mountains can attest to how influential the moon light can be and how much you can see when it's out.

I was tired and before I knew it I was asleep. I woke

early, it was still dark out and after looking at my watch I discovered it was just past 3am. I don't know why I was awake, but I had a sense something I woken me. I laid there and tried to fall asleep but what happened next prevented me from falling back to sleep at all the rest of the night.

A loud smack sounded on the side of the house.

I sat up and listened.

Another loud smack came.

It was on the side of the house where the rock and the trash stealer had run too.

I crawled over to the front window and looked down, but now the moon had set and I couldn't see a thing.

I was spooked. I didn't know what to think. I wasn't a Bigfoot person so I wasn't aware at the time if they liked to hurt humans. I then wished I had brought my Smith & Wesson inside with me. Stupidly I had left it in the glove compartment of my truck.

I recalled there were some two by fours which had been cut down to four foot lengths and planned on using one of those as a weapon.

Another loud smack came.

This time it made me jump. I was officially scared and didn't know what to think. I'm not a small person, I stand around six feet tall, but what knowledge I had of a Bigfoot was they were huge and no doubt strong.

I leaned against the bare sheetrock and listened as it smacked the side of the house over and over. It would pause about a minute between smacks. I then heard a howl in the forest about fifty or so yards away behind the house.

All I could think was, "Oh, shit! There's another one." I don't know why I found that odd. Did I just assume there was only one Bigfoot?" It's funny to think back on now, but I was terrified of one, now I might be dealing with two.

I white knuckled the 2x4 and prayed that these things would just go away, but my prayers wouldn't be answered so easily.

A house under construction carries sound and when I heard the front door knob jiggle I almost pissed myself. I quickly tried to recall if I had secure it and I had, I gave myself a pat on the back and prayed more that these things wouldn't try to break in.

The jiggly stopped and was replaced by a loud slap now on the opposite side of the house, this slap prompted another howl, this time it was closer.

I was legitimately fearful for my life and began to question whether I should make a run for it and hopefully drive off unscathed. It took me about ten seconds to discount that idea. I was locked inside and I had the high ground so to speak, by going out I was exposing myself.

A few more loud slaps came but no howl in response.

I then heard something messing with my truck. I again crawled to the front window and looked out but I couldn't really make anything out. It was this that I realized how lucky I was that I had the sense about me not to run, because I may have run right into them. By the sound it seemed like they were tapping on the windows and trying the doors to see if they'd open, they didn't because I locked them. Old habit from high school. You're thinking, why did he lock his truck, he's in the middle of nowhere. Like I said, old habit I developed after having my truck broken into in high school.

For what must have been thirty or so minutes I could hear two distinct foot patterns around the house moving about. From my truck, back to the front door, the back door, the garage, around the house several times, and then it stopped.

I waited thinking the sound would return but it didn't. I made my way down in the dark, I didn't want to turn the lantern on for fear of giving away my location in the house. I arrived at the front door, placed my ear against it only to jump back when one of the creatures smacked the door. I can't recall, but I might have pissed myself a little there.

There was a creature of unknown origin and size just on the other side of this knotty alder door. Only some wood separated me from possible certain death. I think I moonwalked back like Michael Jackson and ran up the stairs. Again, I don't know what I was thinking. If this thing or things wanted me they could easily break down this door and come get me.

Another thirty minutes passed with no sound. I wondered if they were there. I was tempted to go back downstairs, but I decided against it. I stayed up in the bedroom, back against the wall listening. I did this until I fell back asleep.

I woke to the sun's rays hitting my face. I jumped to my feet, looked out the window to see some of my stuff strewn around near my truck and some other materials from the work site tossed about. I went downstairs and looked around, but there was no sign of anything. I got the nerve up to go out and there I found dozens of tracks all around the house.

I decided then and there I was done for the day. I packed up my stuff and left.

I retuned the next day when the other crews were there, but during the night it had rained and the tracks that had been left were washed away. I thought about telling the other guys, but chose not to. Being made fun of for something as fanciful as possibly seeing a Bigfoot doesn't win many friends and / or future work.

In fact this is the first time I'm telling anyone about it. I know it's not as exciting as other people's encounters, but it was scary, really really scary.

Thanks again for allowing me to share. All the best.

CHAPTER 10
THE SCARECROW MAN

(I am telling a story my grandfather told me many times, in his own words.)

I grew up in an old farmhouse in the middle of nowhere in Indiana, United States. We had no neighbors nearby and back when I was younger we didn't have running water or electricity either. We had an outhouse and it was a time similar to the great depression. Food was scarce and sometimes, when the family was hungry, we had to go out into the woods and try to kill our meal. We would walk for a few miles through the woods until we came to a cornfield. We knew it had to belong to someone because it was well taken care of and the corn grew in perfectly but we would steal it. It was only a few cobs and only so we wouldn't starve but something happened to me one night when I went into that cornfield that I will never forget and it still haunts my nightmares. Sometimes, when I'm all alone and it's dark in the bedroom, right before I fall asleep, I can see him at the foot of my bed and he reaches out his arms to me, his fingers twitching. It haunts me when I'm awake as well.

My name is Hank and aside from being dirt poor, I had a very happy childhood. Everyone where we lived was poor back then so it isn't like we were outcasts or anything different from everyone else we knew. My brother and I used to spend all day playing in the woods behind the house and we never got bored. We saw some strange things but never as bad as the night I snuck into the cornfield to steal a vegetable for dinner. My brother had gone with my father to see if they could catch something, even if it was a rabbit or a squirrel my mom would make it taste like steak and anything was better than starving. We weren't religious and I didn't believe in ghosts or the paranormal, at least not up until that point. I was twelve years old and while my mom never asked me to steal anything, she would mention how she would love a vegetable with the meat and that, I knew, was my cue to take a hike and go grab some corn. There wasn't anything else except corn for as far as the eye could see and the cornfield was almost directly connected to the woods which was mighty uncommon.

Though I wasn't superstitious at all, that cornfield always gave me the creeps. That night I knew I had to go alone and I was so nervous I actually prayed the whole way there. I kept thinking someone was following me but every time I looked back there was no one there. I heard them walking and I even thought a few times that I heard them breathing heavily too. I had about an hour to get to the cornfield, grab four ears of corn from the very back, and make my way back through the woods to get back home. It would usually take me and my brother, walking at a normal pace, about half that time. I was walking really fast though because it was dark, I didn't have a flashlight and I was really scared. The moon was full and I couldn't shake the odd sensation that someone was following me.

Finally I stopped and yelled to see if anyone was there. I thought that maybe my brother had decided to tag along with me after all and was trying to get his kicks by watching me sweat with anxiety. I yelled for him to come out. There was a patch of the woods that was just very tall grass and come to think of it, it was very much out of place. Everywhere else you would look there were trees and some trails but in that one spot, it was only the tall grass. I was about five feet, two inches tall at the time. I hadn't had my growth spurt yet but the grass was twice as tall as I was. Something told me to just keep right on going and not to look back. I couldn't move though and was in the throes of some sort of panic attack unlike anything I had ever known before. I was breathing heavily and my mouth was dry from hanging open the way it was. I just stood there and stared. It looked a little bit like a man, standing thee in the tall grass. It had red hair and its head almost reached the top of the grass, it had to have been more than ten feet tall and massively wide. Its head was gigantic but seemed to be proportionate to its body. I couldn't see anything but the face and it looked sort of like a human being but also it looked sort of like a primate. It had reddish brown hair and it growled low at me. It was looking directly at me and I was looking right back at it. Its eyes were black and soulless and the creature, whatever it was I didn't know, looked angry. It sniffed the air.

I don't know what I was thinking but I picked up a long stick and threw it at the thing, yelling at it to get away from me and to go back where it came from. I swear it roared at me and the trees all around me shook as the ground below me rumbled. I was literally almost knocked off my feet. Then something even more unbelievable happened when it grew even taller right before my eyes. I didn't know that it had been crouching in the tall grass the whole time and it was even taller than I had originally thought that it was. It was at least thirteen feet tall once it stood up and terror gripped me. I stood there, slack jawed and bug eyed as it growled at me again. It moved very quickly for how big it was and it was most certainly faster than I was. It moved behind one of the trees that was in the path of the way I was headed to the cornfield. It peeked out from behind it. I threw another stick, a bigger one that time. It pounded on the tree and roared again. I didn't know what else to do. My mother was never going to believe me that I couldn't get to the cornfield because this massive half man/ half ape thing was blocking my path. I ran right past it and didn't look back. I heard it smashing into the trees as it ran after me. It was so fast I don't know how it didn't catch me but after only about a minute or two of running away, it wasn't behind me anymore, of that I was sure. I was already so frightened of the cornfield and now I had to deal with knowing that something was just lurking somewhere, waiting for me to make my way back through the woods on the way home. I didn't see any good looking corn in the back and normally my brother and I would have to walk into the middle a little bit to get the good ones. There was a scarecrow there, or at least, that's what it looked like at first.

I walked hesitantly over to the scarecrow and looked up at it. It had on very strange clothes for a scarecrow, at least as far as what I had always seen. It seemed too like its clothes had been changed since the last time I had been there which I figured had been about a month. I heard a gunshot and nearly peed my pants. It was more than likely my dad and/or my brother killing our supper and then I really knew I just had to get the corn home. Suddenly the scarecrow turned and looked down at me. It had an evil grin on its face and coal black eyes. It still looked like a scarecrow but it was moving, coming down off the pole to try and grab at me. He wore a clean and freshly pressed gray suit. His mouth was twisted in an evil grin and it was everything a little kid in the country's nightmares are made of. I screamed and that's when the owner of the property where the corn was came outside and fired his shotgun in the air. He yelled for me to get the hell off of his property before he called the law. He didn't see me, of course but he had to have noticed corn was always missing. Come to think of it, maybe he hadn't but had just sensed that someone was out there. I guessed he didn't notice his scarecrow was missing right then either. I turned to run but the scare-crow man was behind me and I ran right into him. He didn't grab me or anything but he started pinching my arms and laughing like a lunatic. His face was cartoonish and hellish, demonic and jovial, all at the same time. I yelled for it to let me go, and it did.

I grabbed some corn absentmindedly because, even with everything I had experienced already, I was still mindful of how my daddy's belt buckle would feel on my bare behind when I got home if I didn't have the corn with me. I grabbed four, shoved them in my pack and ran. The scarecrow was laughing and giggling like an excited school girl the whole time behind me. I suddenly didn't hear it anymore and when I looked back he was back on his pole, clean suit and all. It was like he was never real in the first place. I was crying, had wet myself and still had to deal with the human/primate beast in the woods that I was sure was waiting for me. I walked slowly and kept my eyes open. Every single noise was surely the beast, according to my adrenaline filled and overactive mind. I wiped my eyes and my nose on my sleeves. I heard a lot of rustling and even some jogging near where I was walking but I tried not to think about it and figured I would just give it the corn should it try to attack me again. Nothing happened though, on the way back in the woods. When I got home my parents immediately knew that something was wrong.

I told them what happened, leaving out the part about the animated scarecrow. I did tell them about the other thing and my father knew right away that I had encountered something he called Sasquatch. I hadn't ever heard the word before but he was excited about it. I cleaned myself up, we had our meat and corn for dinner and my brother and I went to bed. The next morning my father wanted me to go with him and show him where I had seen the beast. I cried and pleaded and begged for him not to make me but he told me to stop being a wuss and to man up. I grabbed a shotgun and went with him to the little clearing patch of very tall grass. He looked around all on the ground and sure enough there were footprints there. They were about nineteen inches long and about nine inches wide. I was immediately terrified but my father whooped and howled with joy. He was convinced if he caught one he would be famous, at least locally, and that our problems would be solved for a little while. I didn't know it then but my father was ahead of his time. The craziest part was that I knew it was there, somewhere and probably up in a tree, watching us. I didn't want my father to kill it but not because I wanted to show it any kindness or mercy, no. I wanted to be able to walk through the woods in peace and not have to deal with however many of them were out there who would be angry at the death of the one I had seen. We searched those woods for hours that day but never found anything. My dad was disappointed and eventually we inadvertently ended up in the cornfield.

I immediately looked over at the scarecrow and it was in a raggedy old pair of blue coveralls with a dirty white shirt underneath. It had a straw hat on and it looked perfectly ordinary. A little creepy but like I said they always creeped me out in the first place. It was still broad daylight so my dad and I went back to the house to wash up for dinner. We talked the whole way about other things and my dad was alright by the time we got back home and he seemed to be over the whole thing. We ate dinner and everything was normal. I went into the woods many times after that and into the cornfield as well. I never saw anything strange again but I thought I caught glimpses of the Sasquatch, if that's what it was, out of the corner of my eyes from time to time but it never approached or confronted me ever again and I have no idea why. That first night I had been sure it wanted to devour me but I have come to learn, through years of research, that they're simply very territorial and sensitive to a human being laying eyes on them. I don't know what Bigfoot is but I think it's a sort of elemental like a fairy or something. I believe they come and go from this plane or dimension as they please. It also makes sense to me that they would avoid us human beings like the plague because of how the initial reaction is almost always to go and hunt it with guns and other weapons. We are to the point now of trying to prove its existence but it's already been proven to me. As for the man in the suit in the cornfield, I have absolutely no ideas who or what that was. Maybe it had something to do with the full moon but he still haunts me and I would see him from time to time near the outhouse when it was dark and in the middle of the night. He would stand behind one of the trees and put out his fingers like he was looking to pinch me again. My brother claims to never have seen the entity or the Sasquatch but the bruises it left on me were real and took a longer time than usual to heal. I was touched by the paranormal and the supernatural that night but that was the end of it for the most part. The scarecrow man never touched or approached me again and once I moved out of that house with my parents, I've only ever seen him again in my nightmares. It feels good to finally get this all out and I hope whoever reads this will understand that sometimes things we cannot explain just happen and we aren't meant to know why or how. We are simply meant to live with it and deal with it however we are able to. But, that's just one really old man's opinion. My two cents won't make you any richer so feel free not to take it if you'd like.

CHAPTER 11
IT GRABBED MY LEG

My encounter happened in 1997 in the middle of nowhere, Oklahoma. My family didn't have a lot of money so most of our vacations were spent camping in the woods. I was thirteen at the time and I didn't mind because I loved the woods. That year it was just going to be me and my parents because my older brother had gone off to college the year earlier. It was the end of August and the last fun thing I was going to get to do before school started up again. I had spent my life in the woods, basically, and I was familiar with all of the animals in the region. I knew all the normal sounds of nature and I had also gotten to know what wasn't normal. I was a bit of a nerd and loved facts and research so every time before we would go camping, I would bone up so to speak on my knowledge of the area we were going to. It wasn't always the same place though it was always in Oklahoma. That year we were going to some new spot my dad had heard about from a friend at work. It was much further off grid so to speak than any of the other places we had gone and I was happy about that. I was always expected to try and "make friends" with other kids who were camping or otherwise around the areas where we went and I was awkward. I was looking forward to it and we left on a Friday with nothing but ten whole days of being out in the middle of nowhere with no one else around but us. Even the hour-long car ride there flew by because of how excited we all were.

We had to park our car in some trees and hike out to the campsite. We hiked for about forty minutes before my dad found a spot he thought was acceptable and there was a large water source nearby for fishing and swimming. I should have been relaxed and feeling good by the time we got there. Despite how tired I was though it was like I couldn't let my guard down. From the time we entered those woods right after we had parked the car, I could not relax and enjoy myself. My beautiful and outgoing mother had the voice of an angel but instead of singing with her along the trails like I usually did, I kept feeling the need to look over my shoulder and keep watch on what was going on around us. It must have been evident in my lack of responses when my parents were talking to me because eventually, once we started setting up the tents, my dad asked if everything was okay. I smiled and told him I was fine but I felt anything but. There was a very eerie feeling in those woods but because my parents hadn't seemed to notice, I tried my best to shake it off as just my overactive and juvenile imagination. I couldn't shake it though and by the time night time rolled around and it was dark outside, I found myself sweating and my body shaking, and it had nothing to do with the chill in the air or the heat blazing off of the giant fire my dad had going. We roasted some s'mores and told our usual scary stories but no matter how hard I tried, I just couldn't relax. I kept not only feeling like we were being watched but I kept hearing little rustling noises coming from the surrounding woods. Now, normally those sounds wouldn't have been unusual but it sounded like it was something much bigger than your average animal that would be running around that close to human beings and their campfire. It sounded big, whatever it was and I felt a malevolence in the air that I couldn't possibly explain and therefore didn't try to. Eventually and much to my relief my parents were tired and decided to call it a night. We were going to get up early and go fishing and swimming and I was hoping that by that time, and after a good night's sleep, I would feel refreshed and much better. I knew if I couldn't shake those feelings that it was going to be an extremely long trip for me.

That night I had a hard time falling asleep and kept feeling like there was something right outside of my tent. I didn't hear anything other than the rustling that I had been hearing all night. This sounded much closer and whatever it was sounded larger than I had initially thought. You know the sound a snake makes as its body slithers through some thick brush? That's what I kept hearing except it sounded like a human sized snake. I don't even know really if that's what I was hearing or if it's something I kept imagining in my head. I tossed and turned and eventually I looked at my watch and it was one in the morning, three hours after we had all initially laid down. I was in a small, single tent and my parents were in a double right opposite of me. They were mere feet away but I felt like I was all by myself all of a sudden. I started feeling claustrophobic in my tent and needed to get out and get some fresh air. I went to the bathroom in some nearby trees and as I turned to walk back to my tent I thought I felt something brush up against my bare ankles. I only had on my boxer shorts and a pair of slip on sandals. I jumped and looked down immediately but didn't see anything except some tall grass and laughed at myself for being such a scaredy cat. However, as soon as I took one step, something did reach out from that bush and overgrown grass and grab me. It wrapped around my ankle and yanked me down to the ground before I had even been able to register what was happening. I turned around while I was on the ground because I had fallen on my stomach. I was sitting up then, still with whatever that thing was wrapped around my one ankle and trying to drag me away with it. To where, I still don't know but I do know what I saw, it's burned into my memories and something I see in my nightmares still to this very day.

It was a hand, but not a human one. The fingers were at least twice the size of a human being's and it was a dark gray color. The fingers were gnarled and looked a little disjointed but the grip it had on my leg was strong and no matter how much I wiggled and squirmed, I couldn't get it to let me go. The knuckles were huge and all I could see that was connected to the hideous looking hand was a bit of an arm. The arm was extremely thin, again it looked too thin to belong to a human being, and it was the same color gray. The skin looked leathery and spotted, and like it was peeling off in clumps in some places. The rest of the arm and whatever was attached to it seemed to be hiding inside of the thick and overgrown brush underneath the tree. I took all of that information into my brain in a matter of mere seconds and then I started to scream for my mom and dad. I kicked and pulled but couldn't get it to release its grip on me. Finally I took my other foot and started smashing my heel down on top of the hand and arm and I heard a very loud, very angry sounding hissing noise as it released me and slowly disappeared back into the trees. I jumped up and ran back inside of my tent. Then it finally dawned on me that my parents hadn't come running when I was screaming for them and flashes of them having already been carried away were running through my mind. I got out of my tent and peeked into the sky pocket of theirs. They were sound asleep and somehow didn't hear me screaming at the top of my lungs and fighting that strange thing off, even though they were only about twenty feet away from where it had all just happened. I ran back into my tent and sat there with my knees up to my chest for I don't even know how long. I was shaking and crying and eventually I looked down to see where the thing had grabbed me. I couldn't believe what I was seeing.

It looked like I had been burned. There were finger marks there, and in fact it looked just as if someone had grabbed me and wrapped their fingers around my ankle but the skin was raw and bubbling as though I had gotten some sort of chemical burn or something. It didn't hurt and I even touched it with one of my fingers but it still didn't feel like anything was wrong at all. I felt like, at least if for nothing else, they would serve as proof I wasn't lying when I told my parents about it all at breakfast. I was still very scared but the adrenaline and fear must have been too much because I fell asleep rather quickly after that. I didn't get up to go to the bathroom or for any other reason again that night and in fact I slept right through until I smelled bacon cooking. I opened my eyes and the sun was brightly shining. I could hear my mom and dad giggling about something as they made breakfast and was reluctant immediately to tell them about what had happened to me the night before. They hadn't been getting along with each other for a really long time and it seemed like they were finally enjoying each other again. I somehow knew how important that was, even at that young age, and decided not to tell them. I took one more look at my ankle but of course, there was nothing there. I was so well rested at that point I had begun to think I had merely imagined the whole thing the night before and knew for sure at that point that I wouldn't be telling my parents about it. I might tell them once we were home, but I wasn't going to bring it up to them and ruin their good time together. I put on the biggest smile I could and got out of my tent to have some breakfast.

I said good morning to my parents in my most cheerful voice and we ate and laughed together. Eventually it was time to go to the stream but I still felt like we were being intently watched the whole time and no matter what I did or how hard I tried, I simply couldn't shake off that feeling. I tried not to let it show and neither one of my parents even seemed to notice. I tried to forget about it and just have fun and for the most part it worked. About an hour into our swim my father realized he had forgotten something we needed back at our camp and my mom wanted to walk back with him. There was no one else around and probably wasn't for miles and they asked me if I would be okay by myself for a little while because they were going to go, grab the item and come right back. I must've looked nervous because my mom offered to stay with me but before I could answer my father decided I would be fine and told me not to move and they'd be right back. I smiled and said okay and watched them disappear into the woods. The second they were out of my sight the entire forest went quiet and something happened that I don't understand to this day. There was no sound at all.

I couldn't even hear the sounds of the water splashing as I moved around in it and even tried jumping into the water to see if it would make a sound but it didn't. There was a slight humming in the air but it wasn't so distinctive as to be overwhelming. I froze in place as I watched some of the bushes surrounding the water part, the whole while thinking something was going to come walking out and grab me again. That didn't happen but I was far too nervous to stay in the water and had decided to just sit down on a rock and wait for my parents to get back. I started to swim towards the rocks so I could pull myself out and that's when something grabbed my ankle and started pulling me down into the water. I instantly panicked and every time I would get myself back up to the surface, I would barely be able to catch my breath. Remember there was no sound, including that of my own splashing so I knew that my screams weren't going to be heard by anyone. I could hear myself screaming but it felt far off, like someone screaming through a shield a mile away. Finally I was able to break free and got out of the water as fast as I could. I ran away from it and that's when I finally saw the whole creature that belonged to the arm and hand that had grabbed me the night before and that I was absolutely sure had just tried to pull me under the water and draw me right there too. It came slithering out of the water and it was looking right at me.

It looked almost like a human being but it was that dark gray color and looked like it had leather and beat up skin. It was peeling and chunks were falling off as it slithered slowly on its stomach and made its way towards me. I could do nothing but stand there and watch as I slowly kept backing away from it. It had two legs, two feet, two arms and two hands with those abnormally long fingers. The nails were long, yellowed and sharp which was something I hadn't noticed the night before. It had one long arm and hand reaching out to me. Its mouth was wide open and it had no teeth. In fact its mouth was extremely and unnaturally wide open and I just kept thinking of a snake the whole time. It had gigantic black eyes, similar to what we commonly attribute to the gray aliens nowadays but it was not an extraterrestrial, at least not fully, and it wasn't fully human either. It kept staring at me as it came towards me and my trance was only broken when from behind me I felt someone grab me and at the same time heard my mother scream in horror. My dad yelled that we needed to get out of there and we all turned and ran. We heard an inhuman scream coming from behind us and as we ran back to our camp I noticed the sounds were back and the woods were alive again. My mother kept asking my father what that was but my dad just kept repeating that we had to get out of there immediately. We didn't argue. We packed our things as fast as we possibly could and ran most of the way back to where the car was parked.

On the way home my mother and I kept trying to discuss what we had all seen but my father started getting mad and told us to cut it out and stop discussing it before we somehow called it to us and it ended up at our house. We were quiet but from that day on my mother and I often discussed it in private, never having actually found out what it was that we saw that day. I eventually told her about how it had grabbed me the night before and she was just horrified. I still don't know what it was but I've never been able to swim in anything where I can't see the bottom and still to this day won't even go near any other water. I've since been camping and hiking and have spent a lot of time in the woods. That's mainly due to the fact that my dad was so stubborn he refused to accept what we had seen and kept forcing us back into the woods. We never went back to that particular spot again and I've never seen the creature again except in my nightmares.

CHAPTER 12

IT JUST STARED AT ME

I lived just north of Salt Lake City, Utah most of my life and have spent a considerable amount of time in the woods and forests, both hunting, fishing, hiking, and camping. During these many years being outside in the bush, I have never encountered any that has scared me more than when I saw a grizzly. Yes, what I saw on the day I'm about to detail was scarier than a grizzly.

I was 19 years old when my life would change forever. I was about to go on a mission for the Church of Jesus Christ of Latter Day Saints. I was excited but I also knew I'd miss home so I scheduled to go on a day hike. There is a canyon no more than ten minutes from where I live. It's called American Fork Canyon. I had to go with my two friends but they cancelled last minute. Not one to be deterred and needing my forest fix as I like to call it, I geared up and went out.

I hit the trailhead with a plan to hike for at least five hours. This was going to be my last for about two years here so I wanted it to be a good and difficult hike. There was a single track trial which was about ten miles in length and went around a lake. This would not only provide good exercise but promised to be a gorgeous hike.

I had made it half way and decided to take a break. I broke out my lunch and began to eat. I then heard a faint eerie whistling noise. I didn't think much of it, maybe thinking it was some kind of weird bird in the trees. Maybe I was close to its nest and I was bothering its family. I should note, it was a far off distant sound, but as I continued to eat, the sound grew closer and closer and was now coming from just behind a bush about thirty yards away. It was around then that I caught a whiff of something foul. It was the distinct odor of bad BO, sewer, and skunk like musk. I then felt like something was watching me. Those of you who have spent enough time in the woods and are present know this sensation and that's a good way to say it, it's a distinct sensation that someone has eyes on you.

I felt really uncomfortable and lost my hunger. I packed up my food, threw on my pack and was planning to move on. I couldn't shake the feeling. I got back on the trail but stopped when something started crashing towards me. I froze in fear. I stood and just listened as what sounded like a tornado ripped through the woods, snapping branches and carrying on. Within the matter of seconds this thing appeared on the trail. Right in front of me about thirty feet away was this HUGE, hairy, and powerful looking monster. I know now it was a Sasquatch, but the first word that ever came out of my mouth when I told my friends later was, monster.

It easily stood close to eight feet and its stature was broad and wide. I got a good look at it and I can tell you with certainty that it was a female because I could see its breasts. It huffed a few times, its wide nostrils flared and kept on going in the direction it had been when it crossed paths with me. Before I go on, let me describe in greater detail what I saw. I'll use the correct pronoun, she, as, like I said, it was a female. She was tall, broad and her hair was a blackish brown. The thick long hair was matted with tufts of moss, mud, and twigs in it. Her face was wide, the skin on her face was tannish, like a like brown and she had a thick brow which covered her deep set eyes. What I could make of her eyes were they were black in color. Her arms hung low, almost to her knees and her legs looked thick and powerful. When she pivoted and walked off, it was fluid, more so than I imagined something as big as it could move.

I stood, my heart was pounding, for a long time before I got the nerve to keep going. My hike back was not as enjoyable as the hike in for obvious reasons. I drove to my friend's house and told him right away. He believed me. Together we drove to my other friend's house and I detailed to him the face to face encounter. He was annoyed and disappointed. He had always been a Sasquatch believer unlike me, actually, I wouldn't say I wasn't a believer, I just didn't really have an opinion. Well, I do now and I can tell you, my hand on the Bible, they exist.

CHAPTER 13
WHAT IN THE HECK IN A ZOOBIE?

The following isn't an encounter I had but an interesting set of short stories about a creature known as the Zoobie which supposedly calls Southern California home. I thought you might find this interesting.

~

THE STORY of Zoobies in the San Diego, CA area started in the early 1960s with two teens, a boy and a girl, getting a flat tire while driving through Proctor Valley late at night. The boy pulls to the side of the road under a tree, gets out to look at the damage, his girlfriend becomes fearful when she hears a struggle, so she locks the doors, and the next thing she hears is a scraping on the roof of the car. When cops rescue her in the morning, she learns that the scraping sound was her boyfriend's fingernails. He was dead and hanging by his feet from a tree branch, with big, animal-like footprints around the car.

It should be noted that the nearby Viejas Indians have a legend of a similar creature that guards its burial grounds giving the encounter above and the one below some historical context that corresponds to other native tribes describing Sasquatch or other cryptids.

~

THE NEXT STORY occurred in the 1970s and was taken from a local sheriff's report:

A local psychiatrist claims to have seen a Bigfoot-type creature in the hills near his house. He described a 6 to 7-foot-tall, hairy creature accompanied by two similar critters. He made a plaster cast of a footprint 16 inches long and 8 inches wide. He also related many strange happenings and sounds around his home. Park rangers and other investigators could never confirm the sightings, but plenty of campers, area residents, and even a sheriff's deputy claim to have seen some large, hairy thing tromping the hills of Alpine.

When interviewed by deputies, the psychiatrist called the creature a Zoobie or that's what the deputy thinks he heard.

The doctor described the Zoobie as a large, upright, walking hairy creature and claimed he had three separate encounters with them.

One sighting was made by his entire family within the confines of his yard and immediate area, and at one time they saw three Zoobies. What the doctor described was what he assumed was a father, mother and child with the largest of the Zoobies being over 6 feet tall, maybe 7 feet tall. The tallest was very hairy with a much larger-frame than an ordinary man. What he described as the mother was about 5 feet tall, and the smaller one was about 3 or 4 feet tall.

The doctor had purchased the home from a German couple. The first set of circumstances was the doctor finding damage to the house when he'd just moved in. All of the light bulbs, inside and out, were the yellow bug repellent type. He said the German man told me that he shouldn't change them to white, that he should get used to the yellow light. The doctor asked the German couple if there was an insect problem and the German couple was very evasive about that, – evasive also about a lot of details regarding the house and property. No sooner after having changed the lights did the property suffer damage.

The property did have some acreage with fruit trees in the front and back yards and a picket fence along the perimeter. The doctor complained often that his fruit was being picked off the trees. And what was odd was it was being picked from the top, not the bottom. The trees were upward of 7 or 8 feet high, or maybe 10 feet high. Anyway, the fruit was disappearing from the tops of his trees and his fence was getting knocked down.

He had a wind chime at one of the doors made of brass or some kind of strong metal which frequently rang in the blowing wind, and at one point the wind chime suddenly turned up flattened.

The doctor did make a plaster cast out of one print he found and turned it over to the sheriff's department, nothing came of it.

According to Ken Coon, a former Los Angeles police detective, who visited the Alpine area in 1971, said the doctor's "Zoobies" left v-shaped, 4-toed footprints which were 16 inches long and 8 inches wide with the widest measurement across the toes. The foot narrowed down to 5 inches at the heel.

One of the sightings involved three Zoobies, sighted by the whole family. They had made it a habit to never go out after dark, but one night the doctor's young son went out to call in their pet dog.

In the dark the boy thought he saw the dog near a corner of the house and called out to It. Well, the dog came running back, but from a different corner, and what at first they thought was the dog turned out to be the smaller Zoobie. Apparently it had been laying down and it got up and stood and walked the opposite way, joining the other two, the larger male and female, and they all walked off into the brush.

The doctor was firm that it wasn't an ape or gorilla. It was something totally different. One of the stranger stories happened when the doctor got home after dark one night. They had chickens there, and earlier he'd called his wife to say he was going to be late and to remind her to feed the chickens before night fall, which she did. When the doctor got home he had to exit his car to open the gate. He said that when he went to close it he heard a very low, very guttural voice say, "Here chicky, chicky, chicky..."

It wasn't his wife or anyone in his family as he

found them in the house when he got there. He found that vocalization very disturbing.

It was the doctor's opinion, and we had no reason to doubt him, that the Zoobie had some type of intelligence and the capability of producing sounds like speech. The impression was that one of the creature's was imitating the doctors wife who'd called in the chickens earlier.

There was no more official reports from the doctor or his family, but some locals who knew him state they continued to have encounters the entire time they had the farm. Upon selling it, it is said to have been developed.

CHAPTER 14
THE YENALDOOSHI HAD US

I didn't know what to call my encounter because what we experienced that night can be called by so many different names. So, I'll let you all decide what it was. I was eighteen years old and enjoying my first few months of not being under my parents guardianship anymore (even though I still lived in their house, but that's an eighteen year old's logic, right) and decided to go on an overnight camping trip with my girlfriend in an area near where we lived at the time in New Mexico that was a good and cheap place to be able to do so. I picked her up and we went to the place but immediately noticed it was really deserted. There were hardly any other cars there when we pulled in and when I asked the security guy at the gate about it he leaned in and whispered something about the skinwalkers. I was a little freaked out and thought it was weird that an employee of the camping site would be talking about skinwalkers, especially in an area like where we were, and thought it was no wonder no one was there. Everyone in New Mexico knows you don't talk about skinwalkers, you're not even supposed to think about them and most of the time it isn't just the natives who feel that way. It's sort of just ingrained in the culture. My girlfriend's family lived on a reservation though and she was really put off by it and even a bit angry. I tried to laugh it off because I wanted to make sure it didn't ruin our first overnight together. We hadn't been allowed to stay at one another's houses overnight because we were both minors. She turned eighteen six months before I did and my birthday was three months before we had this encounter. Neither of our parents would let us spend nights together at our houses, but at least we were able to go out for the night without them saying anything. I wanted the night to be special and I made sure to try and keep her mind off of the fact that the idiot at the gate had mentioned the unmentionable. I could tell she was scared but we did our best to distract ourselves.

After we ate and set up our little camp we sat by the fire and just talked about life. Normally we would have told scary stories but I could tell she was too freaked out. She believed that even someone just mentioning skinwalkers to or around you would make you susceptible to them either coming for you or overtaking you altogether. Instead, I put the fire out after a while and we just laid there and looked at the sky. The stars were bright all over the sky and the moon was round and full. It was like heaven, being there on that cool night in the middle of nowhere and all alone. I had been camping my whole life but my girlfriend had only been a few times and like I said this was our first time camping together. I had a large tent that would sleep two people and eventually we decided to call it a night. She seemed to be in better spirits and feeling better and for that I was really glad. There had been an area with actual public restrooms back by the main entrance but we had hiked out pretty far and weren't anywhere near them at that point. It would have taken at least ten minutes to get there and ten to get back and in the dark that could be really dangerous. We had been using the nearby woods and that's where she went in order to use it one last time before bed. I had to go too and so we each went on opposite sides of the camp in order to give each other privacy. As I was finishing up I heard what sounded like a whooshing noise coming from where my girlfriend was but when I called out and asked her if she was okay, I didn't get a response. It sounded to me like something being dragged through the trees. I didn't think much of it at the time and just went back to the tent to wait for her. I could hear her rustling around in the bushes and knew she would be right back. I didn't want to turn off the flashlight until she was done and had made it back safely.

I saw her flashlight go out by where she was standing and shined my light in that direction, figuring it would help her in case she needed to see. I thought her battery had died or something. She immediately whispered loudly for me to turn it off, I listened to her and flicked it off. My girlfriend walked slowly back to the camp and I noticed she was only wearing a t-shirt and her underwear. That was odd to me because we were both brought up in very religious households and we were both very strong in our faith. While we definitely struggled with temptation, we had the talk before and both decided we wanted to wait until marriage. I know that sounds insane nowadays but it was the seventies and it wasn't that unheard of back then, not really and not where we were from anyway. I asked her what she was doing and she just said she was hot. Her voice sounded a little deeper than normal and I asked her again if she was okay. She said she was, again in the deeper, more raspy sounding voice, and I just shrugged it off.

We laid down next to each other and cuddled and she asked me if I would rub her back. I said okay and started to rub it for her. The sounds she was making were animalistic and I didn't understand what was happening. I told her she was making me feel uneasy and asked her one more time if she was okay. She turned to look at me and her green eyes were almost blazing as she told me she was fine and that I needed to quit asking her. I was immediately taken aback because my girl-friend's eyes, though hazel, were normally bright blue. I was a little nervous but then just thought it had been my imagination and that my adrenaline was pumping extra because of the way she was dressed and how she had sounded. Then, she sat up and did something that scared the crap out of me. Well, it wasn't what she did, it was more what she said that scared me. She sat up and hugged her knees into her chest, covering both with the t-shirt, and started talking about how she couldn't believe the security guard had brought up the Yenal-dooshi. Now, Yenaldooshi is not what the guy had said and that's a word specific to one of the local tribes, not the one her family was affiliated with, but it's another word for skinwalker. I knew there was no way in hell she was going to ever bring that up and even on the small chance that she did bring it up she would have used something else to describe it. She wouldn't have used the word skinwalker, let alone another, more specific name for it. I backed away as I sat there. Her blue eyes being bright green, the way she was (un)dressed, how she had asked me to touch her intimately by rubbing her bare back under her shirt and the way her voice changed; it made me start to think that something supernatural was happening but my hormones were making it so that i couldn't put my finger on what it was.

I asked her to pray with me. She hesitated and looked away but she tried to sound nonchalant when she said she would. I grabbed her hand and hung my head in prayer. I started praying out loud and she was suddenly shaking like a leaf. I looked over at her as she yanked her hand away from mine and she looked really pissed off. She looked almost feral. She asked me, again in that deep and strange voice, if we could just go to sleep. I said okay but knew there was something super-natural at play. I wasn't as familiar with the specific legends and lore like she was but I knew a lot about the devil and how he works. I can't lie, I was terrified and had a feeling something wasn't right with my girlfriend. With how suspicious I was though it never occurred to me the scope of what was actually happening until a little later on. My girlfriend once again cuddled up against me and I put my arm around her and started praying again. I was only praying in my head but she jumped up and told me, in a very low and almost inhuman voice, to cut it out. I asked her what she was talking about and then I heard someone calling my name from the nearby woods beyond the tent. My girlfriend seemed to perk up at this and a look of rage and hatred crossed her face. She did the most terrifying and insane thing next. She crawled out of the tent and, while still on all fours, proceeded to run into the woods. I jumped up and yelled after her but the response came from behind me. It was my girlfriend. I was instantly terrified and backed away from her.

I yelled for her to get away from me and started making the sign of the cross. She laughed but when she saw that I was serious she became immediately concerned. She was wearing pajama shorts and a t-shirt. She was no longer in her underwear. I told her to let me see her eyes and she did, they were blue, just like I had remembered them. Her voice sounded perfectly normal too and there wasn't a feral look about her anymore. I started sobbing. She immediately clung to me but I flinched and told her I didn't know if I could trust her. She told me to tell her what had happened and I did. She was scared then too. She explained she had gotten her monthlies and had no choice but to walk in the dark to the restrooms in order to get something to take care of it. I'm trying to keep this as decent as possible so I do apologize but it's a crucial part to the story. She had yelled to me that she was just going to run there fast and come right back and she did say that she wondered why I had only followed her halfway then had turned and left her there, wordlessly nonetheless. She thought she had done something to anger me. I was so confused and honestly, so was she. We both knew what had really happened but we were both too terrified to mention it. We laid there in the tent all night, both of us hardly sleeping, and once the sun rose we packed up our things and got out of there. So much for our romantic weekend together. On the way out the a-hole security guard was there and asked us why we were leaving so soon and it took all of my strength not to punch him in the face. I leaned in and whispered in his ear one word, "yenaldooshi." He pulled back from me, his eyes wide with fear, as I sped off back in the direction towards my house.

My girlfriend and I were both really upset and worried that somehow the creature would be able to get to us while we were at home too. We believed that the guard had somehow brought or led it to us, probably completely by accident, when he mentioned it to us when we first got there. We also believe that at first the entity, the skinwalker, was planning on attacking my girlfriend while she was in the bathroom area or at least on her way there but she said she saw other people both there at the place and also on her way to it. The scent of her blood probably didn't help. It must have noticed she wouldn't be alone and so it changed its mind and transformed or shifted into her image in order to try and seduce me. It wanted me to break my sacred vows and therefore give up my promise to and possibly my faith in my religion and everything she and I believed in. Of course we had no way of knowing and weren't even able to discuss it further because we were both so afraid of bringing it back to us again. I spoke to my mother about it and she convinced me, as my girlfriend's family did for her when it came to me, that our relationship was tainted because of the encounter and that we should stop seeing each other immediately. I know it's hard for a lot of people to understand unless you are as enmeshed in superstition and legends and even religion as she and I were back then. We remained friends and we even attended each other's weddings.

Aside from when I talked about it with my mother that one time, I never told anyone about this. I highly doubt my girlfriend did either because she was actually forced to go and see one of the healers on the reservation once she finally admitted to her family what had happened. I wonder if this is going to bring it back to me somehow. That girl and I are still friends and we are both still very reluctant to speak about it, either with one another or with anyone else. However, lately I've been having nightmares of that night and I see her being attacked and ripped apart and also, I see it in the tent with me. I see it under the guise of being my sweet girlfriend and ripping me apart as well. I don't know what it all means and maybe I'll bring it up the next time I see her. I've since gone through a lot with my religious beliefs but at the end of the day I think that only made the two of us and our chaste relationship more tempting. I don't for one minute believe that religion was the bottom line at all. That jerk at the guard station brought it up and then it smelled her blood. Who knows how many other people who were there that night, before or since, camping or otherwise in those same exact woods who have encountered that same type of evil. It takes many different forms and werewolves are actually the most common sight around those parts to this day. They always have been. Anyway, that's my story and it still baffles, amazes and terrifies me all at once. I'm not sure what to do with all of that. I have other encounters with other entities in the woods I'm going to write out now as well. Thanks for letting me get this out there and I hope it doesn't bring the evil to anyone reading this. Maybe it's best they don't read it while out in the woods anywhere, although, if you're reading this now, it's probably too late. Sorry.

～

CONTINUE THE SERIES WITH
FEAR IN THE FOREST, VOLUME 3

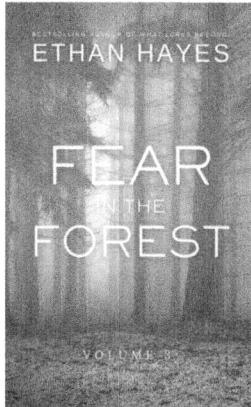

About the Author

Ethan Hayes grew up in Oklahoma and moved to Texas when he attended Texas A&M. Upon graduation he was hired by Texas Parks and Wildlife and remained there until he retired twenty-two years later. He currently lives in southeast Texas with his wife and two dogs. When he's not spending time enjoying the outdoors and writing, he sips a cold beer on his front porch while listening to Bluegrass music.

~

Send in your encounter story:
encountersbigfoot@gmail.com

Also by Ethan Hayes

ENCOUNTERS IN THE WOODS SERIES

VOLUME 1

VOLUME 2

VOLUME 3

VOLUME 4

VOLUME 5

VOLUME 6

VOLUME 7

VOLUME 8

WHAT LURKS BEYOND SERIES

VOLUME 1

VOLUME 2

VOLUME 3

VOLUME 4

VOLUME 5

VOLUME 6

VOLUME 7

VOLUME 8

<u>FEAR IN THE FOREST</u>

VOLUME 1

VOLUME 2

VOLUME 3

VOLUME 4

VOLUME 5

VOLUME 6

VOLUME 7

VOLUME 8

Printed in Great Britain
by Amazon